CW00665315

Description of Summer and Winter Views of the Polar Regions

The copy filmed here has been reproduced thanks
to the generosity of.

Library Division
Provincial Archives of British Columbia

The images appearing here are the best quality
possible considering the condition and legibility
of the original copy and in keeping with the
filming contract specifications

Original copies in printed paper covers are filmed
beginning with the front cover and ending on
the last page with a printed or illustrated impression, or the back cover when appropriate All
other original copies are filmed beginning on the
first page with a printed or illustrated impression, and ending on the last page with a printed
or illustrated impression

The last recorded frame on each microfiche
shall contain the symbol → (meaning "CON-
TINUED"), or the symbol ▽ (meaning "END"),
whichever applies

Maps, plates, charts, etc , may be filmed at
different reduction ratios Those too large to be
entirely included in one exposure are filmed
beginning in the upper left hand corner, left to
right and top to bottom, as many frames as
required The following diagrams illustrate the
method

L'exemplaire filmé fut reproduit grâce à la
générosité de

Library Division
Provincial Archives of British Columbia

Les images suivantes ont été reproduites avec le
plus grand soin, compte tenu de la condition et
de la netteté de l'exemplaire filmé, et en
conformité avec les conditions du contrat de
filmage

Les exemplaires originaux dont la couverture en
papier est imprimée sont filmés en commençant
par le premier plat et en terminant soit par la
dernière page qui comporte une empreinte
d'impression ou d'illustration, soit par le second
plat, selon le cas Tous les autres exemplaires
originaux sont filmés en commençant par la
première page qui comporte une empreinte
d'impression ou d'illustration et en terminant par
la dernière page qui comporte une telle
empreinte

Un des symboles suivants apparaîtra sur la
dernière image de chaque microfiche, selon le
cas le symbole → signifie "A SUIVRE", le
symbole ▽ signifie "FIN"

Les cartes, planches, tableaux, etc , peuvent être
filmés à des taux de réduction différents
Lorsque le document est trop grand pour être
reproduit en un seul cliché, il est filmé à partir
de l angle supérieur gauche de gauche à droite
et de haut en bas, en prenant le nombre
d'images nécessaire Les diagrammes suivants
illustrent la méthode

1	2	3

1
2
3

1	2	3
4	5	6

128

2 2,5

ROYAL PANORAMA,
VIEW OF THE

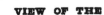

SUMMER.	
1. Remarkable appearance of the Sky.	3. "Investigator."
2. Enormous Iceberg.	4. Crow's Nest.
	5. Stupendous Glacier.

WINTER.	
	3. " Investigator,"
	4. Snow Wall.
1. North East Cape.	5. Beacon erected on North East Cape.
2. Trapping White Foxes.	6. Leopold Harbour.

Printed by W. J. Golbourn, 6, Princes Street, Leicester Square.

LEICESTER SQUARE.
POLAR REGIONS.

6. Tops of land seen through the glacier.
7. Bear Hunting.
8. Singular Iceberg.

9. Captain Ross.
10. "Enterprise."
11. Boats preparing to tow the vessels.

7. House and Beacon on Whaler Point, to the right
   of which is seen a remarkable floating Iceberg.
7 a. Aurora Borealis.
8. Captain Bird.

9. "Enterprise."
10. Carrying Provisions to Whaler Point.
11. Observatory.
12. Cape Seppings.

15 p. *(handwritten annotation)*

DESCRIPTION

OF

SUMMER AND WINTER VIEWS

OF THE

POLAR REGIONS,

AS SEEN DURING THE

EXPEDITION OF CAPT. JAMES CLARK ROSS, KT. F.R.S.

In 1848-9,

NOW EXHIBITING

AT

The Panorama, Leicester Square.

PAINTED BY THE PROPRIETOR,

ROBERT BURFORD,

ASSISTED BY H. C. SELOUS,

FROM

DRAWINGS TAKEN BY LIEUT BROWNE, OF H.M.S. "ENTERPRISE."

And Presented to Mr. Burford by the Admiralty.

London:

PRINTED BY W. J. GOLBOURN, 6, PRINCES STREET, LEICESTER SQUARE.

1850.

PRICE SIXPENCE.

NW
998
B953d

THE POLAR REGIONS.

In order to increase the interest, and at the same time to give a more comprehensive view of those extraordinary regions of everlasting ice and snow, under different aspects, the present Panorama has been divided into two distinct subjects, one-half the great circle exhibiting the Polar seas at midnight in the summer season, the other presenting a similar scene at noon, under all the sublime severities of an arctic winter.

The summer portion of the Panorama, to which the spectator is first introduced, represents the Expedition in the month of July, in what was named Glacier Harbour, on the coast of Greenland, in latitude 73° 42' N., longitude 55° 20' W., " threading their way as they best could through lanes of water in the ice, which extended to the very verge of the horizon, and was thickly studded with bergs of great size." Desolation here reigns triumphant ; all is wild disorder. The sea, piled into solid mountains of ice, strangely mingles its white pinnacles with the dark and frowning summits of rock that here and there rise to an immense height ; and the earth, buried beneath its cumbrous load of frozen water, blends its dreary shores, undistinguishable by any boundaries, with the bleak deserts of the ocean ; all seems one continued and vast pack of ice in close array,—a sublimely picturesque scene, of which there exists no parallel. Towering ice-bergs of gigantic size and the most fantastic shapes ; immense hummocks ; huge masses of ice formed by pressure ; columns, pyramids, and an endless multitude of singular forms, heaped together in the wildest disorder, threatening each moment, as they are driven in mighty strife by the wind or tide, to crush the ships to atoms. In some parts huge stalactites are gracefully pendant from the larger masses ; others present sparry crystals and brilliant icicles, exhibiting a thousand nameless effects of light and shade, arising from proximity or distance, the prominent surfaces being tinged with vivid emerald and violet tints, whilst in clefts, crevices, and deep recesses, lurk shades of the most intense blue, strikingly contrasting with the alabaster-like fabrics by which they are surrounded. At the distance of about three miles, rises an immense and imposing barrier of ice, a vast glacier, the supposed line of the coast of Greenland, beyond which are again plains and rugged wastes of ice, whilst a remote line of mountains are seen along the horizon, in some parts in considerable length, without interruption ; in others abruptly broken off for a short space, and again resumed ; the whole forming a sublime and splendid exhibition of icy grandeur.

43386

4

Towards the south the horizon is overspread by an arch of bright and splendid crimson light, tinging the ice and snow in the direction of its rays with a warm and beautiful colour; and the whole scene is illumed by the sun, which shines in these regions with a dazzling splendour unknown to the inhabitants of a more southern climate.

The winter scene presents most prominently the two ships in their winter quarters in Port Leopold, firmly beset by the ice, in a position nearly north and south; the housings of the decks and all upon them white with snow; the masts, tops, shrouds, stays, and every portion of the rigging that was left standing, on which a particle of snow could lodge, encrusted with a fleecy covering, presenting if not a very cheerful, at least a most picturesque and beautiful appearance. The ice here is a perfectly flat surface, being covered several feet in depth with snow, the harbour being only distinguishable from the land by the line of rocks by which it is surrounded, which, towards its entrance, rise to an immense height, forming two noble capes, the bare and precipitous sides of which present strata of primitive limestone, mostly horizontal, sometimes piled with great regularity, at others so confused as to make it evident that they mark some great convulsion of nature; their dark frowning masses singularly contrasting with the dazzling whiteness of the snow. Around in every direction the distance is one interminable waste, and desolate region of eternal winter, like unfinished portions of the creation from which man and his interests seem for ever banished; whose very barrenness is beautiful, but whose vast solitude conveys a feeling of total privation and utter desolation.

Towards the south the hemisphere is splendidly illuminated by that extraordinary and beautiful phenomenon, the Aurora Borealis,—vividly darting its brilliant coruscations towards the zenith, and tinging the snow with its pale mellow light. The moon, also, which shines with peculiar brightness, presents one of those remarkable phenomena so frequently seen in these regions. The remaining portions of the sky are clear, dark, and unclouded; studded with numberless stars of peculiar lustre, which, with the refraction from the snow, renders anything like a deep or positive gloom of rare occurrence.

Both views form striking and romantic scenes, most difficult to conceive, the awful grandeur and sublimity of which cannot be contemplated without intense interest and enthusiastic admiration.

The great and important problem of a north-west passage from the Atlantic to the Pacific, which has engaged the interests of the curious, and provoked the inquiries of the learned for many centuries, and has especially occupied the attention of the British Government, who, for a considerable period have zealously and steadily pursued the inquiry, seems as far from being solved as ever it was; but it has become quite clear, that discovery has already been pushed far beyond the limits of practical utility, and that for all purposes of commerce or traffic, the Arctic regions must remain a sealed book to the human race, until some vast change shall occur in the temperature and in the meteorological arrangement of the globe.

The present voyage of Sir James Clark Ross was not undertaken for making new discoveries, nor for scientific purposes alone, but to seek for and render assistance to the Expedition, consisting of H. M. ships the "Erebus" and "Terror," under the command of Sir John Franklin, which sailed from England on the 19th of May, 1845, for the safety of which considerable fears were felt.

The Expedition, consisting of H. M. ships "Enterprise," Capt. Sir J. C. Ross, and the "Investigator," Capt. Bird, sailed from the Thames on the 12th of May, 1848, and after a boisterous voyage, stopping a few days at Whale Island, arrived at Upernavik, a small Danish settlement on the east side of Baffin's Bay, on the 6th of July, where the ice was found to be so closely packed as to obstruct for several days any further advance. On the 13th they were again able to proceed, and on the 20th, standing in shore to the eastward, among numerous islets, forty-five miles within the boundary line of the west coast of Greenland, as laid down in the present charts, an immense glacier was observed extending completely along the imaginary coast line, apparently formed between high and unconnected land, as seen in the first portion of the Panorama. The ships, from the immense pack of loose unconnected ice, here became almost unmanageable, and were violently whirled about, being in great danger of being nipped; the "Enterprise" having two of her boats injured, one, a cutter, being completely squeezed together. There is, perhaps, no danger more great, no difficulty more perplexing, than that of commanding a vessel through the intricate mazes of the ice, whose vast fields, meeting in headlong fury, driving, whirling, and dashing each other to pieces, form a scene appallingly frightful, perilously grand.

On the 26th, the ships were off the three islands of Baffin, whence, continuing their course, as Sir James observes, "under varying circumstances of perplexity, anxiety, and success," they passed, with considerable difficulty, across Melville barrier; but the movement of the pack was so much impeded by calms, or light and uncertain winds which prevail during the summer months amongst drift ice, that it was not until the 20th of August, that during a heavy breeze from the north-east, they, with all the sail they could carry, bored through a pack of ice of moderate thickness, which it was necessary at all hazards they should pass, and gained clear, or, what is called by Polar navigators the "west water," in latitude 75½ N., fortunately without sustaining any very severe damage.

The ships then steered for Pond's Bay, and there the real business of the Expedition commenced. Land was made on the 22nd, ten miles to the southward of that place, and the line of the main pack of ice was traced close in against it, at the distance of three or four miles, so closely pressed home, as to leave no room for ships or boats to pass between it and the shore. Every point of this coast, which was known to be the summer resort of the Esquimaux, was carefully examined, as was also the coast to the northward, but without a single human being having been seen. On the 26th, when off Possession Bay, a party was sent on shore to search for any traces of Sir J. Franklin having touched at this general point of rendezvous, but nothing was found but a paper left there by Capt. Parry, in 1819, which, although much damaged, was clearly deciphered.

On the 1st of September the Expedition arrived off Cape York, where a party was sent on shore to explore, and to fix a conspicuous signal, in which was placed a cylinder containing papers for the guidance of any party that might fall in with it, a service performed with much skill, under difficult circumstances, by Lieut. McClintock. The weather had now become stormy and foggy, but still the ships were pushed forward, despite all obstacles; guns were discharged; rockets and blue lights fired; and casks were each day thrown overboard, containing notices that a depôt of provisions and other necessaries would be found at Cape Leopold, which place, the appointed rendezvous, it now became necessary for the Expedition to make as soon as possible, a course of considerable difficulty and danger, from the immense quantity of ice, which Sir James was of opinion was greater than had ever before been seen in Barrow's Straits at so early a period of the season.

On the 11th of September the ships entered Port Leopold harbour, a spacious and commodious bay, with excellent groundings, good depth of water, and a sandy bottom, situated on the northern extremity of the west shore of Prince Regent's Inlet. Fortunate was it that the right moment was chosen, for Sir James says:—"Had we not got into port that day, it would have been impossible to have done so any day afterwards, the main pack having during the night closed the land, and completely sealed the mouth of the harbour. We had now," he continues, "accomplished one very material point, and were rejoiced to find the anchorage, of which we had before been in much doubt, well adapted to our purpose. I resolved, therefore, that it should be the winter quarters of the 'Investigator,' whilst the steam launch should proceed westward, in search of a harbour for the 'Enterprise.'"

It, however, shortly became certain, from the early setting in of winter, and the unbroken state of the ice, that it would be impossible to reach Melville Island, and the pack at the harbour's mouth preventing immediate departure, all hands were set to work, to land with the greatest despatch three months' provisions from each ship, on Whaler Point. These operations were still incomplete when, from the significant appearance of the young ice, it became necessary to turn attention to the ships. A quantity of heavy ice had drifted into the bay, and collected in their neighbourhood, and the young ice was making rapidly over, when a prevalence of easterly winds caused the pack to press so heavily against the outer margin of the harbour ice, that the ships were carried away with their anchors so far up towards the head of the bay, that they grounded at low water, and it became necessary for the crews to cut a channel in the ice forty feet wide, to warp them off the shore; this had scarcely been accomplished, when another severe pressure drove them again into shallow water, and had they not been hauled off in time, it is probable they must have laid aground all the winter. The work of cutting was recommenced, and after two or three days, they were again got into a position of comparative safety,

ft there
clearly

, where
;nal, in
of any
h skill,
er had
orward,
lights
notices
md at
ecame
rse of
f ice,
e been

our, a
pth of
of the
right
t that
vards,
letely
ccom-
ge, of
se. I
vesti-
1 of a

inter,
reach
diate
patch
pera-
f the
ntity
hood,
terly
f the
ur up
nd it
wide,
when
they
ound
two
fety,

although with only a foot or two of water to spare at low tide; the winter now, however, set in with so much severity, that it was impossible to keep the men any longer so employed without serious injury to their health.

On the 12th of October, the ships were finally hove into their winter position, within 200 yards of each other, and were soon firmly frozen in, and surrounded by an immense field of level ice, as seen in the winter portion of the Panorama. "Although I could not but feel extreme disappointment," remarks Sir James, "at the small advance we had been able to make during our first season, we had much to be thankful for in having been permitted to gain secure winter quarters at Port Leopold, a position that, of all others, was the most desirable, if any one spot had to be selected for that purpose, being at the junction of the four great channels of Barrow's Straits, Lancaster Sound, Prince Regent's Inlet, and Wellington Channel. It was hardly possible for any party, after abandoning their ships, to pass along the shores of any inlet without finding indications of the proximity of our Expedition."

In this inhospitable region, isolated for a period from the rest of the world, these heroes of the Arctic Seas passed 342 days, during three whole months of which they never caught a single glimpse of the joyous sun; all was alike night, that luminary having disappeared below the horizon on the 9th of November, and having been entirely lost to sight from the ships, until the 9th of February. The thermometer at the same time fell so low as 40°, 50°, and on one or two occasions, even to 60° minus, the average reading during the three months being 35°.

Sir James observes, " the winter was passed as are all winters in this climate, but long experience and liberal means gave us many comforts that no other Expedition had enjoyed, yet it is remarkable that the health of the crews suffered more during this winter than on any former occasions. Our want of success might have tended in some measure to depress their spirits, and unfortunately the cold of winter was prolonged unusually far into the spring, before we could give them active employment."

No language can convey an adequate idea of the sadness and dreariness of such a situation, surrounded on all sides by the same desolate and cheerless prospect, with no sound breaking the universal monotony, but the roaring of the tempest, or the occasional cracking of the ice; but it requires no very lively imagination to conceive the frightful tedium endured during the many hours of darkness, in the close and confined space below decks, a space that had been purposely shorn of its due proportions, partly to admit of the insertion of double timbers to strengthen the ships, partly for the heating apparatus to keep up such a temperature as was consonant with existence, and partly to make room for the immense amount of provisions and stores each ship carried. The greatest hardships and privations were necessarily severely felt, not indeed whilst there was anything to do, but it was in the midst of stillness, inactivity, ill health, and failing hopes, that the sharpest trials and the most intense sufferings were experienced. In alternations between the clammy atmosphere below and the keen pinchings of the cold air above, into which they were unable to move without being covered with an immense load of clothing, and

8

even then at the risk of being frost bitten, one day being scarcely distinguishable from another, save by extra tediousness or discomfort, that the crews were compelled to wear out existence, during these three long dreary months of darkness. What prison could be more dreary? With what joy they beheld the return of light, for the most hazardous duty was a change for the better, and any change was a benefit, as it roused them from the torpor of their spirits, and the stagnation of their blood.

So soon as the great severity of the winter had passed, several short preliminary journeys were made, in April and May, to carry out small depôts of provisions to the west of Cape Clarence and to the south of Cape Seppings; and on the 15th of the latter month, Sir James Ross, with Lieutenant McClintock and a party of twelve men, with forty days' provisions, tents, blankets, clothes, and other necessaries, lashed on two sledges, departed to examine all the smaller indentations of the coast, in which any ship might have found shelter. He traversed the north coast of North Somerset, beyond Capes Rennell, Gifford, and Bunney; where, finding the land tend nearly due south, he followed it, over land never before trod by civilized man, being all new discovery, to that part of the coast opposite Kerswell Bay. It had been his intention to reach the magnetic pole, where he had previously been, but owing to some of the party becoming useless from debility and lameness, he was obliged to forego the attempt. Sir James, however, accompanied by Serjeant Hurdich and W. Thompson, a seaman of great endurance, advanced eight or nine miles beyond the rest, to the extreme south point of a small peninsular, latitude 72° 38′ N., longitude 95° 40′ W., from whence they obtained an extensive view, and from the atmosphere being at the time peculiarly favorable for distinctness of vision, observed the extreme high cape of the coast, not more than fifty miles distant. After having traversed nearly 400 miles over the boundless region of ice, mostly at night time, to avoid snow blindness,—an almost unparalleled feat of exploration,—the party returned to the ships on the 23rd of June, after an absence of thirty-nine days, so completely worn out by fatigue, that every man was, from some cause or other, under the doctor's hands for two or three weeks.

During this time, Capt. Bird had despatched parties in several directions. One under Lieut. Barnard, to the north shores of Barrow's Straits; a second, under Lieut. Brown, to the east shores of Prince Regent's Inlet; and a third, under Lieut. Robinson, along the western shores of that Inlet; each party going about fifty miles, and at the farthest point leaving a cylinder under a heap of stones, with particulars of the position of the ships, &c. All the parties were unsuccessful in the main object, and all suffered severely from snow blindness, sprained ancles, and debility.

The season was still extremely backward, there being scarcely a pool of water visible on the surface of the ice, yet Sir James was so anxious to push westward to Melville Island, that all hands that were any way able were set to work to cut a canal through the ice to the harbour's mouth, a distance of more than two miles. A line having been marked by the officers, 15 and 18 feet saws were worked with triangles, cutting, on an average, 200 feet per day, four, sometimes six saws being employed at one time; the ice varying in thickness from 3 to 5 feet. The ships were thus gradually got down to the entrance, where, the pack in the inlet having considerably receded, a motion was created that materially assisted in loosening the ice, so that, on the 28th of August, they got quite clear of the harbour.

The Expedition now attempted to reach the north shores of Barrow's Straits, to examine Wellington Channel, and reach Melville Island; but soon came on a fixed land of ice, that had not melted all the season. Here the ships met with an adventure almost unparalleled in the annals of Polar navigation. A strong wind, which suddenly rose on the 1st of September, brought the loose pack of ice through which they had been struggling down upon the ships, so closely besetting them that they sustained the most severe pressure. There was no escape: skill and ability were of no avail. High ridges of hummocks were thrown up around them, and the temperature falling below zero, the whole was soon formed into one solid mass, extending from shore to shore of Barrow's Straits, and as far to the east and west as the eye could discern from the mast-head: a dismal prospect, as it appeared extremely improbable that it would again break up before winter. It was therefore with a mixture of hope and extreme anxiety, that on the wind shifting to the westward the whole body of ice was observed to begin to drive eastward, carrying with it the ships and the human beings they held, perfectly helpless, in its terrible gripe, at the rate of eight or ten miles daily. They were thus—in the centre of a field of ice more than fifty miles in circumference—taken along for twenty-three days, through Lancaster Sound and beyond Pond's Bay, and having been in this singular manner conveyed so far on their voyage home, at the moment when nothing less than their destruction was expected, their release was almost miraculously brought about by the great field of ice of itself being suddenly rent into innumerable fragments, as if by some unseen power, and all sail being made through the floe, a few hours brought them into open water. It being now too late in the season for further operations, Sir James judiciously determined to return to England, and arrived at Scarborough on the 3rd of November.

Sir James speaks in the highest terms of all associated with him, especially expressing his deep obligations to Captain Bird, for "his cordial co-operation and zealous support;" also, his admiration of the conduct of both officers and crews, between whom the greatest harmony existed. The same spirit of emulation seemed to animate every one: they had to grapple with difficulties of no ordinary nature, and to endure toil and privation, and the perilous incidents unavoidably attendant on such an expedition, which, by skill, daring, and steady perseverance, they triumphantly surmounted. The whole enterprise was nobly and gallantly conducted; nothing was left unattempted that anxiety could suggest or foresight contrive. If it failed, no fault can be imputed to the party under Sir James Ross: the powers of nature overcame the efforts of man, and they were forced to return; not, however, without having performed important services, which may yet be productive of much good. It is the general opinion, that the lost Expedition is not eastward of any navigable point in the Arctic regions; and not a single sign was met with that would lead to the conclusion that Sir John Franklin had experienced any misfortune. They carried provisions for three years, which might be extended to four, or even longer, if they were fortunate in taking seals and birds; if in pressing distress, they would no doubt abandon the ships, and make for the nearest point where they could expect relief, and probably fall in with some of the depôts formed for them. Let us therefore hope that it may please Providence to shield them from the many dangers of their enterprise, and restore them in health and honour to their country. Certain it is that nothing will be wanting on the part of Sir John and his gallant companions, to accomplish all that human means and human intellect can command.

In the mean time, it is highly satisfactory to know, that another Expedition of relief having been resolved upon, no time was lost in refitting the "Enterprise" and "Investigator" for the purpose, and they sailed from Woolwich for Behring's Straits on the 10th of January, under the command of Captain Collinson and Commander Mc Clure.

Mr. BURFORD feels it his duty to state, as an erroneous impression is entertained by some portion of the Public that the Panoramic Views are a species of scene-painting, coloured in distemper, or other inferior manner, that such is not the case—they being all painted in the finest oil colour and varnish that can be procured, and in the same manner as a gallery picture.

Mr. BURFORD also considers it right to say that THIS *is the* ORIGINAL *Panorama, which was first opened about* SIXTY YEARS AGO, *and since that time has been increasing in public favour and attraction until it has reached its present high popularity. With the exception of one, it is the* ONLY PANORAMA IN LONDON, *though various other exhibitions, consisting merely of moving pictures, make use of the term Panorama.*

vigable
th that
ed any
ght be
g scals
on the
ief, and
i there-
i many
iour to
part of
means

Expo-
:fitting
sailed
ler the

ression
Views
nferior
: finest
er as a

IGINAL
ce that
it has
t is the
visting

DESCRIPTION OF THE PLATE.

~~~~~~~~~~~~~~~~~~~~~~~~~~~~

SUMMER VIEW.

No. 1.—*Remarkable Appearance of the Sky.*

This splendid arch of crimson light is a phenomenon peculiar to the Arctic Regions, and always appears in a direction opposite to the sun.

No. 2.—*Enormous Iceberg.*

The vessels were secured to this enormous berg by hawsers and ice-anchors, and were constantly in the most perilous situations, in danger of being nipped by the vast masses floating about, or of being crushed by the overturning of the bergs,—a circumstance of frequent occurrence, involving very great danger. During the night (which was a very fine one) that the ships were moored to this berg, the awful silence that prevailed was several times broken by the overturning of bergs, and the fearful crash occasioned by masses of ice detached from the glacier falling into the sea.

No. 3.—*"Investigator."*

A vessel extremely well fitted for the service. She was built at Greenock, and launched January, 1848; she was then towed to the Thames, and strengthened at Green's yard at Blackwall, under the inspection of Mr. Rice, a gentleman from Plymouth, who had superintended the equipment of former expeditions. The "Investigator" is 340 tons burden, 118 feet in length, 28 feet beam, 6 feet in height on the mess deck, and draws 15 feet water. She is barque-rigged, and is protected from any violent pressure of the ice, by solid sponsons, or chocks, projecting about three feet; and about the bows, by a sheeting of plate iron. Her figure-head represents the head and shoulders of a walrus. On each side are fitted three pairs of wooden davits, to which were hoisted two cutters of 25 feet length, three whale-boats, and a dingy; over the stern was the captain's gig, and on board, between the fore and main masts, was stowed the pinnace—a boat, 31 feet in length, 10 broad, and of 10 tons burden, fitted with a ten-horse power locomotive engine. Internally she was in every way similarly fitted as the "Enterprise." She was commanded by Capt. Bird; and the crew consisted of 15 officers, 18 petty officers, carpenters, 22 able seamen, 3 stewards, and a sergeant, corporal, and 6 privates of the Woolwich division; in all, 67 persons, of which number three seamen died during the winter.

No. 4.—*Crows' Nest.*

This ingenious observatory, which is much in use amongst the northern whale fishers, is said to have been invented by the elder Captain Scoresby, to watch the motions of the fish. It consists of an open barrel, fixed to the maintop-gallant mast-head, in the bottom of which is a trap door, approached by a ladder of ropes, with wooden bars for steps, instead of ratlins. It forms a safe look-out in all weathers, leaving the hands perfectly at liberty.

No. 5.—*Stupendous Glacier.*

This immense glacier, the accumulated snow and ice of ages, is about three miles from the ships; it extends for many miles along the supposed coast of Greenland, and in some parts is several thousand feet in thickness. The actual height of the face of the glacier above the sea could not be ascertained, from the enormous masses of recently detached of ice floating about, but it may be estimated at approaching 1,000 feet perpendicular. Old, or lost Greenland, was discovered 983, by some Norwegians, who planted a colony on the eastern coast, which flourished until the fifteenth century, when, by the gradual increase of the ice, it became inaccessible; heavy, consolidated floes, having imbedded in them bergs of vast size, which, grounding, served to fix the whole firmly to the shore, were soon formed into an impenetrable barrier, that has, and doubtless will remain for ages compact and immovable, presenting a rugged, perpendicular front, bidding stern defiance to the roaring of the winds, or the raging billows of the sea, and mocking the vain attempts of man to pass it. The general aspect from one extreme to the other, is barren and rugged; the average elevation is 3,000 feet, there being in some places mountains from 4,000 to 6,000 feet in height. The glacier on the west coast is formed between high and unconnected land as far as could be seen, making it appear, as has been supposed, that Greenland is formed of a vast number of islands. It is named by the sailors the manufactory of icebergs, for every fall of hail and snow increasing its size and propelling it forward, vast overhanging projections are formed by the action of the sea below, the enormous weight of which separating them from the main body, they fall in masses of many thousand tons into the water, with terrific roar, the heaviest portion of course sinking below. Soundings were taken from the ships to the depth of 160 fathoms without finding the bottom.

No. 7.—*Bear Hunting.*

The Polar bear (*Ursus Maritimus*) is too well known to need particular description. In these regions, where it might be supposed so large an animal must necessarily perish for want of food, they manage to support nature on seals and fish. Some persons assert that they sleep during the winter in ice caverns, but it is more probable that they migrate as the winter approaches to the more western parts, in search of open water; they are very frequently seen on icebergs a great distance from land, and are good swimmers, but cannot remain long under the water. They seldom evince a disposition to act on the offensive, unless attacked or driven to bay, when they become very ferocious assailants; they are of great strength and size, weighing from eleven to twelve hundred pounds.

No. 8.—*Singular Iceberg.*

Some idea of the vastness of these masses may be formed, when it is stated, that although many of them have an altitude of at least 300 feet, yet not more than one-ninth of the whole appears above water. It is impossible to contemplate these vast elevations of ice, without reflecting on the enormous power that must have been exerted to rend them from the parent mass,

13

No. 9.—*Captain Ross.*

Sir James Clark Ross is an officer of no ordinary character, whether as regards his nautical skill or scientific abilities: he seems to have been formed by nature for the arduous service to which he has devoted himself; to great physical powers, and a constitution equal to any privations, he unites every mental qualification necessary to constitute the man destined to conduct a great and hazardous expedition. The greater part of his life has been spent in the Arctic and Antarctic regions, having accompanied most of the recent voyages of discovery; he sailed with his uncle, Sir John Ross, in 1818, in the four voyages of Capt. Parry, and again in the last voyage of Sir John in 1829, during which he discovered Boothia, surveyed many hundred miles of the coast, and had the proud satisfaction of being the first to plant the flag of his country on the true magnetic pole of the world. Altogether he has spent fifteen summers and nine winters in the polar regions, and in the various departments of astronomy, natural history, and surveying committed to his care, has always received the most flattering testimonials for zeal and ability.

WINTER VIEW.

No. 1.—*North East Cape.*

A very considerable headland, facing Barrow's straits, on which a beacon was raised.

No. 2.—*Trapping White Foxes.*

During the winter, a great many foxes were taken in traps set for the purpose: they were nearly all white; in size, somewhat smaller than the English fox, with the fur thicker, and the brush much larger. As it is well known how large a tract of country these creatures traverse, they were made messengers, or twopenny postmen as the sailors called them, by having copper collars clenched round their neck, on which a notice was punched of the dates, names, and positions of the ships, and the depôts of provisions; they were then set at liberty, in the hope that some of them might be the means of conveying intelligence to the "Erebus" and "Terror," as the crews of those vessels would be naturally anxious for their capture. Before master Reynard obtained his liberty, he generally afforded the sailors a chase within the snow walls that surrounded the ships.

No. 3.—*"Investigator."*

(For description, see page 11.)

No. 4.—*Snow Wall.*

A wall of snow was built between the two vessels for the purpose of facilitating the communication, by affording shelter from the frequent gales of wind, and the blinding drifts of snow which always accompany them; which were as fine as sand, and so thick that the vessels, although only two hundred yards apart, were imperceptible from each other. The building of the wall was commenced from the bow of each ship at the same time, and progressed so as to meet half-way; it was constructed of blocks of snow, which were cut and shaped by cutlasses and shovels; they were cut of a size so as to enable two men to lift and place them in a proper position. Walls of a similar kind were also constructed round each of the ships, the non-conducting power of which prevented the abstraction of heat, which was considerable in windy weather.

Lightning Source UK Ltd.
Milton Keynes UK
UKHW020710090123
415051UK00009B/802